Grade 5 Handwriting:

Big Kids Writing Practice Edition

SPEEDY
PUBLISHING

Speedy Publishing LLC
40 E. Main St. #1156
Newark, DE 19711
www.speedypublishing.com

I prefer...

_____
_____
_____
_____
_____
_____
_____
_____
_____
_____
_____
_____
_____
_____
_____

I think...

_____

_____

_____

_____

_____

_____

_____

_____

_____

_____

_____

_____

_____

_____

I feel...

I know...

I believe...

In my opinion...

_____

_____

_____

_____

_____

_____

_____

_____

_____

_____

_____

_____

_____

_____

The best thing about...

_____

_____

_____

_____

_____

_____

_____

_____

_____

_____

_____

_____

_____

_____

_____

_____

The greatest part about...

_____

_____

_____

_____

_____

_____

_____

_____

_____

_____

_____

_____

_____

_____

The worst part about...

Everyone should...

_____
_____
_____
_____
_____
_____
_____
_____
_____
_____
_____
_____
_____
_____

If I am a Superhero...

My spooky story...

_____

_____

_____

_____

_____

_____

_____

_____

_____

_____

_____

_____

If you liked...

I am happy when...

_____

_____

_____

_____

_____

_____

_____

_____

_____

_____

_____

_____

_____

....is better than...

My bestfriend...

If I were a...

_____
_____
_____
_____
_____
_____
_____
_____
_____
_____
_____
_____
_____

Dogs...

_____

_____

_____

_____

_____

_____

_____

_____

_____

_____

_____

_____

_____

Cats...

_____

_____

_____

_____

_____

_____

_____

_____

_____

_____

_____

_____

_____

_____

Doctors...

_____

_____

_____

_____

_____

_____

_____

_____

_____

_____

_____

_____

Teachers...

_____

_____

_____

_____

_____

_____

_____

_____

_____

_____

_____

_____

_____

_____

Firemen...

_____

_____

_____

_____

_____

_____

_____

_____

_____

_____

_____

_____

Policemen...

_____
_____
_____
_____
_____
_____
_____
_____
_____
_____
_____
_____

Chocolates...

_____

_____

_____

_____

_____

_____

_____

_____

_____

_____

_____

_____

Vegetables...

_____
_____
_____
_____
_____
_____
_____
_____
_____
_____
_____
_____
_____

Butterflies...

_____

_____

_____

_____

_____

_____

_____

_____

_____

_____

_____

_____

Birds...

_____

_____

_____

_____

_____

_____

_____

_____

_____

_____

_____

_____

_____

_____

Earth...

Fruits...

_____
_____
_____
_____
_____
_____
_____
_____
_____
_____
_____
_____
_____
_____

Made in the USA
Las Vegas, NV
16 October 2021